Jukes-Edwards / A Study in Education and Heredity

A. E. Winship

PREFACE.

Of all the problems which America faces on the land and on the seas, no one is so important as that of making regenerates out of degenerates. The massing of people in large cities, the incoming of vast multitudes from the impoverished masses of several European and Asiatic countries, the tendency to interpret liberty as license, the contagious nature of moral, as well as of physical, diseases combine to make it of the utmost importance that American enterprise and moral force find ways and means for accomplishing this transformation. The grand results of the movement in New York city inspired by Jacob Riis; the fascinating benevolence of the Roycroft Shop in East Aurora, N.Y.; the marvelous transfiguration of character—I speak it reverently—at the George Junior Republic, Freeville, N.Y., added to the College Settlement and kindred efforts merely indicate what may be accomplished when philanthropy supplements saying by doing, and when Christianity stands for the beauty of wholeness and is satisfied with nothing less than the physical, mental and moral conversions of all classes among the masses at home as well as abroad, in the East as well as in the West.

A problem is primarily something thrown at us as a challenge for us to see through it. To solve a problem is to loosen it so that it may be looked into or seen through. Whatever contributes to the loosening of a problem by throwing light upon the conditions is of value in aiding in its solution, hence the publication of this study of the family of Jonathan Edwards as a contrast to the Jukes.

A.E.W.

Somerville, Mass., *June 1, 1900.*

TABLE OF CONTENTS.

CHAPTER I

THE JUKES

Education is something more than going to school for a few weeks each year, is more than knowing how to read and write. It has to do with character, with industry, and with patriotism. Education tends to do away with vulgarity, pauperism, and crime, tends to prevent disease and disgrace, and helps to manliness, success and loyalty.

Ignorance leads to all those things that education tries to do away with, and it tends to do away with all the things that education tries to cultivate. It is easy to say these things, and every one knows they are true, but few realize how much such statements mean. It is not easy to take a view of such matters over a long range of time and experience.

A boy that leaves school and shifts for himself by blacking boots, selling papers, and "swiping" fruit often appears much smarter than a boy of the same age who is going to school all the time and does not see so much of the world. A boy of twelve who has lived by his wits is often keener than a boy of the same age who has been well brought up at home and at school, but such a boy knows about as much and is about as much of a man at twelve as he will ever be, while the boy that gets an education becomes more and more of a man as long as he lives.

But this might be said a thousand times to every truant, and it would have very little effect, because he thinks that he will be an exception. He never sees beyond his own boyish smartness. Few men and women realize how true it is that these smart rascally fellows, who persist in remaining in ignorance, are to be the vicious, pauper, criminal class who are to fill the dens of vice, the poorhouses, and the prisons; who are to be burglars, highwaymen, and murderers. In place of opinions, it is well sometimes to present facts so clear and definite that they cannot be forgotten.

R.A. Dugdale, of New York State, began the study of "The Jukes" family in 1874, and in 1877 in the twentieth annual report of the New York Prison Commission he made a statement of the results. [Footnote: G.P.

Putnam's Sons, New York, reprinted this study in "The Jukes."] This brief summary of "the Jukes" is based upon the facts which Mr. Dugdale has published.

"The Jukes" is a name given to a large family of degenerates. It is not the real name of any family, but a general term applied to forty-two different names borne by those in whose veins flows the blood of one man. The word "jukes" means "to roost." It refers to the habit of fowls to have no home, no nest, no coop, preferring to fly into the trees and roost away from the places where they belong. The word has also come to mean people who are too indolent and lazy to stand up or sit up, but sprawl out anywhere. "The Jukes" are a family that did not make good homes, did not provide themselves with comforts, did not work steadily. They are like hens that fly into the trees to roost.

The father of "The Jukes" Mr. Dugdale styled "Max." He was born about 1720 of Dutch stock. Had he remained with his home folk in the town and been educated, and thrifty like the rest of the boys, he might have given the world a very different kind of family from "The Jukes."

Max was a jolly good fellow and not very bad. He was popular and he could tell a good story that made everybody laugh. Of course he was vulgar, such jolly good fellows are usually vulgar. He would not go to school, because he did not like it. He would not stay in evenings, for he did not like that. He did not enjoy being talked to, but always wanted to talk himself, and to talk to boys who would laugh at his yarns. He would not work for he did not like it. He wanted to go fishing, hunting, and trapping; so he left home early and took to the woods.

Max liked nature. He thought he was lots better than town people because he knew more about nature. He found a lovely spot on the border of a beautiful lake in New York State, where the rocks are grand, the waters lovely, the forest glorious. There was never a more charming place in which to be good and to love God than this place where Max built his shanty about 1750. But he did not go there to worship or to be good. He went simply to get away from good people, to get where he would not have to work, and where he would not be preached to, and this beautiful spot became a notorious cradle of crime. Nature is lovely, but it makes all the difference in the world how we know nature and why we love it.

In 1874 Richard L. Dugdale was employed by the New York Prison Commission to visit the prisons of the state. In this visit he was surprised to find criminals in six different prisons whose relatives were mostly criminals or paupers, and the more surprised to discover that these six criminals, under four different names, were all descended from the same family. This led Mr. Dugdale to study their relatives, living and dead. He gave himself up to this work with great zeal, studying the court and prison records, reports of town poorhouses, and the testimony of old neighbors and employers. He learned the details of 540 descendants of Max in five generations. He learned the exact facts about 169 who married into the family. It is customary to count as of a family the men who marry into it. He traced in part others, which carried the number up to 1,200 persons of the family of the Jukes.

The Jukes rarely married foreign-born men or women, so that it may be styled a distinctively American family. The almost universal traits of the family were idleness, ignorance, and vulgarity. They would not work, they could not be made to study, and they loved vulgarity. These characteristics led to disease and disgrace, to pauperism and crime. They were a disgustingly diseased family as a whole. There were many imbeciles and many insane. Those of "the Jukes" who tended to pauperism were rarely criminal, and those who were criminal were rarely paupers. The sick, the weak, and goody-goody ones were almost all paupers; the healthy, strong ones were criminals.

It is a well-known fact in sociology that criminals are of three classes: First, those who direct crime, the capitalists in crime, who are rarely arrested, who seldom commit any crime, but inspire men to crime in various ways. These are intelligent and have to be educated to some extent. They profit by crime and take slight risks.

Second, those who commit heroic crimes and find some satisfaction in the skill and daring required. Safe-breaking, train robbery, and some types of burglary require men of ability and pluck, and those who do these things have a species of pride in it.

Third, those who commit weak and imbecile crimes, which mark the doer as a sneak and a coward. These men rob hen roosts, waylay helpless women and old men, steal clothing in hallways, and burn buildings. They are always cowardly about everything they do, and never have the pluck to steal chickens even until they are half drunk. They often commit murder, but only when they are detected in some sneaking crime and shoot because they are too cowardly to face their discoverer.

Now the Jukes were almost never of the first or second class. They could not be criminals that required capital, brains, education or nerve. Even the kind of pauperism and crime in which they indulged was particularly disgraceful. This is inevitably true of all classes of people who combine idleness, ignorance, and vulgarity. They are not even respectable among criminals and paupers.

There is an honorable pauperism. It is no disgrace to be poor or to be in a poorhouse if there is a good reason for it. One may be manly in poverty. But the Jukes were never manly or honorable paupers, they were weaklings among paupers.

They were a great expense to the state, costing in crime and pauperism more than $1,250,000. Taken as a whole, they not only did not contribute to the world's prosperity, but they cost more than $1,000 a piece, including all men, women, and children, for pauperism and crime.

Those who worked did the lowest kind of service and received the smallest wages. Only twenty of the 1,200 learned a trade, and ten of those learned it in the state prison. Even they were not regularly employed. Men who work regularly even at unskilled labor are generally honest men and provide for the family. A habit of irregular work is a species of mental or moral weakness, or both. A man or woman who will not stick to a job is morally certain to be a pauper or a criminal.

One great benefit of going to school, especially of attending regularly for eight or ten months each year for nine years or more, is that it establishes a habit of regularity and persistency in effort. The boy who leaves school to go to work does not necessarily learn to work steadily, but often quite the reverse. Few who graduate from a grammar school, or who take the equivalent course in a rural school, fail to be regular in their habits of effort. This accounts in part for the fact that few unskilled workmen ever graduated from a grammar school. Scarcely any of the Jukes were ever at school any considerable time. Probably no one of them ever had so much as a completed rural school education.

It is very difficult to find anyone who is honest and industrious, pure and prosperous, who has not had a fair education, if he ever had the opportunity, as all children in the United States now have. It is an interesting fact developed from a study of the Jukes that it is much easier to reform a criminal than a pauper.

Here are a few facts by way of conclusion. On the basis of the facts gathered by Mr. Dugdale, 310 of the 1,200 were professional paupers, or more than one in four. These were in poorhouses or its equivalent for 2,300 years.

Three hundred of the 1,200, or one in four, died in infancy from lack of good care and good conditions.

There were fifty women who lived lives of notorious debauchery.

Four hundred men and women were physically wrecked early by their own wickedness.

There were seven murderers.

Sixty were habitual thieves who spent on the average twelve years each in lawless depredations.

There were 130 criminals who were convicted more or less often of crime.

What a picture this presents! Some slight improvement was apparent when Mr. Dugdale closed his studies. This resulted from evening schools, from manual training schools, from improved conditions of labor, from the later methods of treating prisoners.

CHAPTER II

A STUDY OF JONATHAN EDWARDS

The story of the Jukes as published by Mr. Dugdale has been the text of a multitude of sermons, the theme of numberless addresses, the inspiration of no end of editorials and essays. For twenty years there was a call for a companion picture. Every preacher, orator, and editor who presented the story of the Jukes, with its abhorrent features, wanted the facts for a cheery, comforting, convincing contrast. This was not to be had for the asking. Several attempts had been made to find the key to such a study without discovering a person of the required prominence, born sufficiently long ago, with the necessary vigor of intellect and strength of character who established the habit of having large families.

In 1897 a professional scholarly organization—to which the author has the honor to belong—assigned to him, without his knowledge or consent, the duty of preparing an essay upon Jonathan Edwards for the May meeting of 1898. The study then begun led to a search for the facts regarding his family, and when it came to light that one of Jonathan Edwards' descendants presided over the New York Prison Commission when it employed Mr. Dugdale to make a study of the Jukes, the appropriateness of the contrast was more than ever apparent.

In this study the sources of information are the various genealogies of families in which the descendants of Mr. Edwards play a part, various town histories and church and college publications, but chiefly the biographical dictionaries and encyclopaedias in which the records of the men of the family are chronicled. It would be impossible to follow out the positions occupied by the various members but for the pride they all feel in recording the fact that they are descendants of Jonathan Edwards. A good illustration of this may be had in the current announcements of the marvelously popular novel, "Richard Carvel," in which it is always emphasized that Mr. Winston Churchill, the author, is a descendant of Jonathan Edwards.

Only two Americans established a considerable and permanent

reputation in the world of European thought prior to the present century,—Benjamin Franklin and Jonathan Edwards. In 1736, Dr. Isaac Watts published in England Mr. Edwards' account of the beginning of the great awakening in the Connecticut valley. Here more than a century and a half ago, when the colonies were small, their future unsuspected and the ability of their leaders unrecognized, Jonathan Edwards "erected the standard of Orthodoxy for enlightened Protestant Europe." Who can estimate the eloquence of that simple fact? Almost everything of his which was published in the colonies was speedily republished in England. Of what other American philosopher and theologian has this been true? Here are a few of the tributes to Mr. Edwards:

Daniel Webster: "The Freedom of the Will" by Mr. Edwards is the greatest achievement of the human intellect.

Dr. Chalmers: The greatest of theologians.

Robert Hall: He was the greatest of the sons of men.

Dugald Stewart: Edwards on the Will never was answered and never will be answered.

Encyclopaedia: One of the greatest metaphysicians of his age.

Edinburgh Review: One of the acutest and most powerful of reasoners.

London Quarterly Review: His gigantic specimen of theological argument is as near to perfection as we may expect any human composition to approach. He unites the sharpness of the scimetar and the strength of the battle-axe.

Westminster Review: From the days of Plato there has been no life of more simple and imposing grandeur than that of Jonathan Edwards.

President McCosh, of Princeton: The greatest thinker that America has produced.

Lyman Beecher: A prince among preachers. In our day there is no man who comes within a thousand miles of him.

Griswold's Prose Writers: The first man of the world during the second quarter of the eighteenth century.

Hollister's History of Connecticut: The most gifted man of the eighteenth century, perhaps the most profound thinker in the world.

Moses Coit Tyler: The most original and acute thinker yet produced in America.

This is the man whose intellectual life has thrilled in the mental activity of more than 1,400 men and women of the past century and a half, and which has not lost its virtue or its power in all these years.

England and Scotland are not wont to sit at our feet even in this day, and yet they sat at the feet of Jonathan Edwards as in the presence of a master when he was a mere home missionary, living among the Indians, to whom he preached every Lord's day.

The birth of fame is always an interesting study. It is easy to play the part of a rocket if one can sizzle, and flash, and rise suddenly in darkness, but to take one's place among luminaries and shine with permanent brilliancy is so rare an experience as to present a fascinating study.

Jonathan Edwards was twenty-eight years of age, had been the pastor of a church on the frontier, as Northampton was, for four years without any notable experience, when he was invited to preach the annual sermon before the association of ministers at Boston. Never since that day have Boston and Harvard been more thoroughly the seat of culture and of intellectual power than then. It was a remarkable event for a young man of twenty-eight to be invited to come from the Western limit of civilization and preach the annual sermon before the philosophical, theological, and scholastic masters of the East. This sermon was so powerful that the association published it. This was his first appearance in print. So profoundly moved by this effort were the churches of New England that the clergymen generally gave public thanks to the Head of the Church for raising up so great a teacher and preacher. Thus was born the fame of Jonathan Edwards.

It is nearly 170 years since then. Science and invention, enterprise and ambition have done great things for America and for Americans. We have mighty universities, libraries, and laboratories, but we have no man who thinks more clearly, writes more logically, speaks more vigorously than did Jonathan Edwards, and we have never had such a combination of spirit and power in any other American. This mastery is revealing itself in various ways in hundreds of his descendants to-day, and it has never ceased to do it since his blood gave tonic to the thought and character of his children and his children's children.

CHAPTER III

THE INHERITANCE AND TRAINING OF MR. EDWARDS

No man can have the intellectual power, nobility of character, and personal grandeur of Jonathan Edwards and transmit it to his children's children for a century and a half who has not himself had a great inheritance. The whole teaching of the culture of animals and plants leaves no room to question the persistency of character, and this is so grandly exemplified in the descendants of Mr. Edwards that it is interesting to see what inheritances were focused in him.

It is not surprising to find that the ancestors of Mr. Edwards were cradled in the intellectual literary activities of the days of Queen Elizabeth. The family is of Welsh origin and can be traced as far as 1282, when Edward, the conquerer, appeared. His great-great-grandfather, Richard Edwards, who went from Wales to London about 1580, was a clergyman in the Elizabethan period. Those were days which provided tonic for the keenest spirits and brightest minds and professional men profited most from the influence of Spencer, Bacon, and Shakespeare.

Among the first men to come to the new colonies in New England was William, a son of this clergyman, born about 1620, who came to Hartford, where his son Richard, born 1647, the grandfather of Jonathan, was an eminently prosperous merchant. Richard was an only son. The father of Jonathan, Timothy Edwards, was an only son in a family of seven. Aristocracy was at its height in the household of the merchants of Hartford in the middle of the seventeenth century.

Harvard was America's only college, and it was a great event for a young man to go from Hartford to Harvard, but this Timothy Edwards did, and he took all attainable honors, graduating in 1661, taking the degrees of A.B. and A.M. the same day, "an uncommon mark of respect paid extraordinary proficiency in learning." This brilliant graduate of Harvard was soon settled over the church at East Windsor, Conn., where he remained sixty-five years as pastor.

13

Who can estimate the inheritance which comes to a child of such a pastor who had been born in a merchant's home. In the four generations which stood behind Jonathan Edwards were two merchants and two preachers, a grand combination for manly and intellectual power.

In this pastor's home Jonathan Edwards was born October 5, 1703. Those were days in which great men came into the world. There were born within fifteen years of Jonathan Edwards a wonderful array of thinkers along religious and philosophic lines, men who have molded the thought and lives of a multitude of persons. Among these intellectual giants born within fifteen years of Mr. Edwards were John Wesley, George Whitefield, Swedenborg, Voltaire, Rousseau, and Hume.

In order to appreciate the full significance of Mr. Edwards' legacy to the world, it is well to study some conditions of his life. It would not be easy to find a man whose surroundings and training in childhood were better than those of Jonathan Edwards. The parsonage on the banks of the Connecticut was a delightful home. His parents and his grandparents were ideal American Christian educated persons. He was prepared for college by his father and mother. He was a devout little Christian before he was twelve years of age. When he was but ten years old he, with two other lads about his own age, made a booth of branches in a retired spot in a neighboring wood, where the three went daily for a season of prayer.

He began the study of Latin at six and at twelve had a good preparation for college in Latin, Greek, and Hebrew, all of which had come from home study. He not only knew books, but he knew nature and loved her. From early childhood to advanced years this remained true. He entered Yale college at twelve years of age. In a letter which he wrote while a college freshman he speaks of himself as a child. Not many freshmen take that view of themselves, but a lad of twelve, away from home at college could have been little more than a child.

He was the fifth in a family of eleven children, so that he had no lack of companionship from both older and younger sisters. The older sisters had contributed much to his preparation for college. They were a never-failing source of inspiration. At fourteen he read in a masterly way "Locke on the Human Understanding." It took a powerful hold on his mind and greatly affected his life. In a letter to his father he asked a special favor that he might have a copy of "The Art of Thinking," not because it was necessary to his college work, but because he thought it would be profitable.

While still in his teens he wrote a series of "Resolutions," the like of which it would be difficult to duplicate in the case of any other youth. These things are dwelt upon as indicating the way in which every fibre of his being was prepared for the great moral and intellectual legacy he left his children and his children's children. Here are ten of his seventy resolutions:

Resolved, to do whatever I think to be my duty, and most for the good and advantage of mankind in general.

Resolved, so to do, whatever difficulties I meet with, how many soever, and how great soever.

Resolved, to be continually endeavoring to find out some new contrivance and invention to promote the forementioned things.

Resolved, never to lose one moment of time, but to improve it in the most profitable way I possibly can.

Resolved, to live with all my might while I do live.

Resolved, to be endeavoring to find out fit objects of charity and liberality.

Resolved, never to do anything out of revenge.

Resolved, never to suffer the least motions of anger towards irrational beings.

Resolved, never to speak evil of any one, so that it shall tend to his dishonor, more or less, upon no account except for some real good.

Resolved, to maintain the strictest temperance in eating and drinking.

Yale in the days of Mr. Edwards was not the Yale of the closing year of the nineteenth century. It has now 2,500 students and has had 19,000 graduates. It had a very humble beginning in March, 1702, the year before Mr. Edwards was born. It began with one lone student. The father of Jonathan Edwards had been greatly interested in the starting of the college. In 1701, Rev. Mr. Russell, of Branford, a graduate of Harvard, as was the senior Edwards, invited to his home ten other Connecticut pastors of whom nine were graduates of Harvard. Each brought from his library some of his most valuable books, and laying them upon Mr. Russell's table, said: "I give these books for the founding of a college in this colony." This produced a profound impression upon the clergymen of Connecticut, notably upon the graduates of Harvard. The first year the college was nominally located at Saybrook, but as there was only one student he lived with the president at Killingworth, now Clinton, nine miles away.

When Jonathan Edwards, a lad of twelve, entered college, there had been, all told, only about fifty graduates. It was during the time that he was a student that the college took the name of Yale. The first year he was there the college was in three places at the same time because of dissensions among the students, and the very small class graduated in two places because neither faction would go to the other place. In all these agitations Mr. Edwards took no part. He simply devoted himself to his studies and followed the line of least resistance so far as taking sides in a senseless controversy was concerned. After graduation he remained at Yale two years for post-graduate work, mostly in theology, and then accepted an invitation to preach for the leading Presbyterian church in New York City; but after eight months he returned to Yale as a tutor and remained two years.

At this time he was very severe in discipline, bending every energy to securing the right conditions for the most and best work. This is what he wrote in his diary when he was twenty-one:

"By a sparingness in diet, and eating, as much as may be, what is light and easy of digestion, I shall doubtless be able to think more clearly, and shall gain time:

1. By lengthening out my life.
2. Shall need less time for digestion after meals.
3. Shall be able to study more closely, without injury to my health.
4. Shall need less time for sleep.
5. Shall more seldom be troubled with the headache."

Mr. Edwards was twenty-three years of age when he was ordained at Northampton as associate pastor with his grandfather Stoddard, then in his 84th year, and the 54th year of his pastorate. Soon after this Mr. Stoddard died and Mr. Edwards became pastor in full charge and remained for twenty-five years. He was a great student and thinker. He rose at four o'clock and spent thirteen hours a day in his study. It is worth while to follow the personal intellectual habits of the man whose descendants we are to study. When he was ready for the consideration of a great subject he would set apart a week for it and mounting his horse early Monday morning would start off for the hills and forests. When he had thought himself up to a satisfactory intensity he would alight, fasten his horse, go off into the woods and think himself through that particular stage of the argument, then he would pin a bit of paper on some particular place on his coat as a reminder of the conclusion he had reached. He would then ride on some miles further and repeat the experience. Not infrequently he would be gone the entire week on a thinking expedition, returning with the front of his coat covered with the scalps of intellectual victories. Without stopping for any domestic salutations he would go at once to his study and taking off these bits of paper in the same order in which he had put them on would carefully write out his argument. In nothing did Jonathan Edwards stand out so clearly as boy, youth and man as in his sacrifice of every other feature of his life for the attainment of power as a thinker.

Mr. Edwards has gone into history as a theologian of the most stalwart character. It is undeniable that he preached the most terrific doctrine ever uttered by an American leader, but this was only the logical result of the intellectual projection of his effort to make sacrifices in order to benefit humanity. As a child he sacrificed everything for health and virtue that he might have influence, and as a man he knew no other plan or purpose in life. His masterpiece is upon the "will" which he developed to the full in himself.

The greatest religious awakening that the Western world has ever known was started in his church at Northampton, not over ecclesiastical differences, or theological discussion but over a question of morality among the young people of the town. It had to do with the impropriety of the young ladies entertaining their gentlemen friends on Sunday evenings and especially of their allowing them to remain to such unreasonable hours. And the issue which ultimately drove him from his pastorate, after twenty-five years of service, by an almost unanimous vote was not one of ecclesiasticism or theology, but of morals among the young people. He insisted upon vigorous action in relation to the loose and as he thought immoral reading of the youth of the town. As this involved some prominent families he had to retire from the pastorate.

The views of Mr. Edwards on pastoral work reveal the singleness of purpose of the man as a student and thinker. He never made pastoral calls. He had no criticism to make of those pastors who had talent for entertaining

17

people by occasional calls, but as he had no gifts in that direction he regarded it advisable to use his time in cultivating such talents as he had. Whoever wished to talk with him about personal, moral or religious conditions found in him a profitable counsellor. In his preaching, which was equal to anything America has ever known, he made no attempt to win his hearers by tricks of oratory or by emotional appeals, though he had a most fascinating personality. He was six feet in height, slender in form, with a high, broad forehead, eyes piercing and luminous and a serene countenance. In the pulpit he was graceful, easy, natural and earnest, though he had little action. He rested his left elbow on the pulpit and held his manuscript in his left hand while with his right he turned the leaves. In him were combined the intellectual and moral vigor which are calculated to make the progenitor of a great family.

CHAPTER IV

THE CHILDREN'S START IN LIFE

The eleven children of Jonathan Edwards had an unenviable start in life so far as their environment was concerned. The oldest was still in her teens when serious trouble arose in the parish at Northampton. Mr. Edwards was pastor at Northampton for twenty-five years, and a more fruitful pastorate or a more glorious ministerial career for a quarter of a century no man could ask. He made that church on the frontier the largest Protestant church in the world, and it was the most influential as well as the best known. There began the greatest religious awakening of modern times. In his church, resulting from his preaching, began a revival which stirred into activity every church in Massachusetts, every church in the colonies, and most of the Protestant churches of Great Britain and Europe.

After this long and eminently successful pastorate, Mr. Edwards preached a sermon about the reading and conversation of young people upon subjects of questionable propriety, which led to such local excitement that upon the recommendation of an ecclesiastical council he was dismissed by a vote of 200 to 20, and the town voted that he be not permitted on any occasion to preach or lecture in the church. Mr. Edwards was wholly unprepared financially for this unusual ecclesiastical and civic action. He had no other means of earning a living, so that, until donations began to come in from far and near, Mrs. Edwards, at the age of forty, the mother of eleven children with the youngest less than a year old, was obliged to take in work for the support of the family. After a little time Mr. Edwards secured a small mission charge in an Indian village where there were twelve white and 150 Indian families. Here he remained eight years in quiet until, a few weeks before his death, he was called to the presidency and pastorate of Princeton, then a young and small college.

The last four years of their life at Northampton were indescribably trying to the children. Human nature was the same then as now, and everyone knows how heavily the public dislike of a prominent man bears

19

upon his children. The conventionalities which keep adults within bound in speech and action are unknown to children, and what the parents say behind a clergyman's back, children say to his children's face. This period of childhood social horror ended only by removal to a missionary parsonage among the Stockbridge Indians, where they lived for eight years. Their playmates were Indian children and youth. Half the children of the family talked the Indian language as well and almost as much as they did the English language.

In the years of aspiration these children were away from all society life and educational institutions, in the home of a poor missionary family among Indians when Indian wars were a reality. When Mr. Edwards accepted gratefully this mission church his oldest child, a daughter, was twenty-two, his youngest son was less than a year old. All of the boys and three of the girls were under twelve years of age when they went to the Indian village, and all but one were under twenty. When their missionary home was broken up five of them were still under twenty, so that the children's inheritance was not of wealth, of literary or scholastic environment, or of cultured or advantageous society. Everything tends to show how completely Mr. Edwards' sons and daughters were left to develop and improve their inheritance of intellectual, moral, and religious aspiration.

In these years Mr. Edwards was writing the works which will make him famous for centuries. One of the daughters married Rev. Aaron Burr, the president of Princeton, then a very small institution. Upon the death of this son-in-law, Mr. Edwards was chosen to succeed him, but while at Princeton, before he had fairly entered upon his duties at the college, he died of smallpox. His widowed daughter, who cared for him, died a few days later leaving two children, and his widow, who came for the grandchildren, soon followed the husband and daughter to the better land.

Mr. Edwards died at fifty-six, and his widow a few weeks later. Both died away from home, for the family was still among the Stockbridge Indians. The oldest son was but twenty, and there were five children younger than he. The youngest son was eight and the other only thirteen. To make the picture more clear it must be understood that to these six orphans, under twenty-one, there came at the time of their father's and mother's deaths two little orphans aged four and two respectively, Sarah Burr and her brother

Aaron. Here was a large family from which father and mother, older sister and brother-in-law had been taken almost at a single blow, with two extra orphans to care for.

And with all this there was no adequate financial inheritance. The inventory of Jonathan Edwards' property is interesting. Among the live stock, which included horses and cows, was a slave upon whom a moderate value was placed. The slave was named Titus, and he was rated under "quick stock" and not "live stock," at a value of $150. The silver was inventoried as a tankard valued at $60, a can and porringer at $47, and various other articles valued at $85. The chief material legacy was his library, which was inventoried as consisting of 301 volumes, 536 pamphlets, forty-eight maps, thirty unpublished manuscripts and 1,074 manuscript sermons prepared for the printer. It was valued at $415.

If Jonathan Edwards did not leave a large financial legacy, he did impart to his children an intellectual capacity and vigor, moral character, and devotion to training which have projected themselves through eight generations without losing the strength and force of their great ancestor. Of the three sons and eight daughters of Jonathan Edwards there was not one, nor a husband or wife of one, whose character and ability, whose purpose and achievement were not a credit to this godly man. Of the seventy-five grandchildren, with their husbands and wives, there was but one for whom an apology may be offered, and nearly every one was exceptionally strong in scholarship and moral force.

We have paused long enough on the threshold of the descendants of Jonathan Edwards. We have seen the estimate in which he was held by his contemporaries at home and abroad, and by close students of the history of his times. We have seen what he inherited and by what training and in what environment he was developed. We have also seen the terrible strain to which his children were subjected in childhood from lack of school privileges and pleasing social conditions. It remains to be seen what kind of men and women these children became with childhood disadvantages, but with a grand inheritance and the best of home training.

Remember the size, ages, and financial condition of the family when the father died—the sons being aged eight, thirteen and twenty—and then consider the fact that the three sons graduated from Princeton, and five of

21

the daughters married college graduates, three of them of Yale and one each of Harvard and Princeton. A man might well be content to die without lands or gold when eight sons and sons-in-laws were to be men of such capacity, character, and training as are found in this family.

They were not merely college graduates, but they were eminent men. One held the position of president of Princeton and one of Union College, four were judges, two were members of the Continental Congress, one was a member of the governor's council in Massachusetts, one was a member of the Massachusetts war commission in the Revolutionary war, one was a state senator, one was president of the Connecticut house of representatives, three were officers in the Revolutionary war, one was a member of the famous constitutional convention out of which the United States was born, one was an eminent divine and pastor of the historic North church of New Haven, and one was the first grand master of the Grand Lodge of Masons in Connecticut. This by no means exhausts the useful and honorable official positions occupied by the eight sons and sons-in-law of Jonathan Edwards, and it makes no account of their writings, of noted trials that they conducted, but it gives some hint of the pace which Mr. Edwards' children set for the succeeding generations. It should be said that the daughters were every way worthy of distinguished husbands, and it ought also to be said that the wives of the sons were worthy of these men in intellectual force and moral qualities.

Contrast this group of sixteen men and women with the five sons of Max and the women with whom they lived. In this group there was not a strain of industry, virtue, or scholarship. They were licentious, ignorant, profane, lacking ambition to keep them out of poverty and crime. They drifted into whatever it was easiest to do or to be. Midday and midnight, heaven and its opposite, present no sharper contrasts than the children and the children-in-law of Jonathan Edwards and of Max.

The two men were born in rural communities, they both lived on the frontier; but the one was born in a Christian home, was the son of a clergyman, of a highly educated man who took the highest honors Harvard could give, was himself highly educated in home, school, and at Yale College, always associated with pure-minded, earnest persons, and devoted his thought and activity to benefiting mankind.

Max was the opposite of all this. There is no knowledge of his childhood or of his parentage. He was not bad, as bad men go; he was jolly, could tell a good story, though they were always off color, could trap unwary animals skillfully, was a fairly good shot; but no one was the better for anything that he ever said, thought, or did. Jollity, shiftlessness, and lack of purpose in one man have given to the world a family of 1,200, mostly paupers and criminals; while Mr. Edwards, who never amused any one, who was always chaste, earnest, and noble, has given to the world a family of more than 1,400 of the world's noblemen, who have magnified strength and beauty all over the land, illustrating grandly these beautiful lines of Lowell:

"Be noble! and the nobleness that lies In other men, sleeping, but never dead, Will rise in majesty to meet thine own."

CHAPTER V

MRS. EDWARDS AND HOME TRAINING

Much of the capacity and talent, intensity and character of the more than 1,400 of the Edwards family is due to Mrs. Edwards. None of the brothers or sisters of Jonathan Edwards had families with any such marvelous record as his, and to his wife belongs not a little of the credit.

At the age of twenty-four Mr. Edwards was married to Sarah Pierrpont, aged seventeen. She had an inheritance even more refined and vigorous than that of Mr. Edwards. She was descended on her father's side from the choicest of the Pierrpont family of England and New England. Her father was one of the most famous of New Haven clergymen, one of the principal founders, and a trustee and lecturer of Yale College. On her mother's side she was a granddaughter of Rev. Thomas Hooker, of Hartford, "the father of the Connecticut churches," and one of the grand men in early American history.

Personally, she was so beautiful and so noble-minded that at the age of thirteen she was known far and near for her Christian character and exceptional ability. While she was still but thirteen and Mr. Edwards twenty, he wrote in a purely disinterested way of the remarkable girl: "She is of a wonderful sweetness, calmness, and universal benevolence of mind. She will sometimes go about from place to place singing sweetly; and seems to be always full of joy and pleasure; and no one knows for what."

Mr. Edwards was desirious of being married when he went to Northampton as associate pastor with his grandfather, Dr. Stoddard. Miss Pierrpont was only sixteen years of age, and she declined to be married until she was seventeen. He insisted, but she persisted in her refusal.

Mrs. Edwards lived in her children. To her husband came honor and glory in his lifetime, but to her came denial, toil and care. At eighteen, this young, beautiful, brilliant wife became a mother, and until she was forty, there was never a period of two years in which a child was not born to them, and no one of the eleven children died until after the last child was born. It was a home of little children. Her husband had no care for the household and she wished him to have none. It was her insistence that he should have thirteen hours of every twenty-four for his study. Whatever may have been the contribution of Mr. Edwards to the inheritance of the family, they owed the charming environment of the home to their mother.

This was a delightful home, as many persons have testified who knew it. I saw recently the diary of the famous George Whitefield, where he wrote that he sometimes wondered if it was not the Lord's will that he should marry, that he might thereby be more useful, and that if it was the Lord's will that he should marry, he wished to be reconciled thereto, but he did hope that the Lord would send him as a wife such a woman as Mrs. Edwards, whom he considered the most beautiful and noble wife for a Christian minister that he had ever known. If there be a more charming tribute to woman than this, I have not seen it.

In view of the character of her children and their great success in life, it may be interesting to know how she brought up the children, of whom there were so many, and for which the schools did so little. This is the testimony of one who knew of her home life well: "She had an excellent way of governing her children; she knew how to make them regard and obey her cheerfully. She seldom punished them, and in speaking to them used gentle and pleasant words. When she had occasion to reprove or rebuke, she would do it in a few words, without warmth and noise, and with all calmness and gentleness of mind. In her directions and reproofs of matters of importance, she would address herself to the reason of her children, that they might not only know her inclination and will, but at the same time be convinced of the reasonableness of it. She had need to speak but once and she was obeyed; murmuring and answering again were not known among them. In their manners they were uncommonly respectful to their parents. When their parents came into the room, they all rose instinctively from their seats and never resumed them until their parents were seated; and when either parent was speaking, no matter with whom they had been conversing, they were all immediately silent.

"Quarreling and contention were in her family wholly unknown. She carefully observed the first appearance of resentment and ill-will in her young children towards any person whatever, and did not connive at it, but was

25

careful to show her displeasure, and suppress it to the utmost; yet not by angry, wrathful words.

"Her system of discipline began at a very early age, and it was her rule to resist the first, as well as every subsequent exhibition of temper or disobedience in the child, however young, until its will was brought into submission to the will of the parents."

It is needless to say that all this added materially to the good inheritance of the children.

CHAPTER VI

CAPACITY, CHARACTER AND TRAINING

In view of what has been learned regarding Jonathan Edwards, his ancestors and his children, his grandchildren might have found some excuse for presuming upon the capacity and character which they inherited. In their veins was the blood of famous lines of noble men and women; the blood of Edwards, Stoddard, Pierrpont, and Hooker was thrilling in their thought and intensifying their character. They had inherited capacity and character at their best, but they did not presume upon it. If ever inheritance would justify indifference to training, it was in the case of the grandchildren of Jonathan Edwards, but they were far from indifferent to their responsibility.

It must be understood that the "family of Jonathan Edwards" includes not only his descendants, but the men who married into the family and whose children became descendants of Mr. Edwards. At first this may not seem the proper interpretation, but there is no other that is legitimate. In the case of the "Jukes" Mr. Dugdale includes in the family both the men and the women who married into the family, but in the case of Mr. Edwards there is no call to include the women who thus came into the family, and it would have magnified the study needlessly.

Until quite recently there has been no way to discover the standing of married women in American life except as we know the social, scholastic, and professional position of their husbands. In most families a son-in-law becomes a representative factor of a family. Therefore, whenever the "Edwards family" is spoken of it includes the sons-in-law, but it does not include the daughters-in-law, nor does it go beyond Jonathan Edwards to include his brothers and sisters or their descendants.

The "Jukes" had no inherited capacity or training upon which they could safely presume. Their only chance lay in nursing every germ of hope by means of industry and education, through the discipline of the shop, the training of the schools, and the inspiration of the church. Did they appreciate this? Far from it. Instead of developing capacity by training, not one of the

27

1,200 secured even a moderate education, and only twenty of them ever had a trade, and ten of these learned it in the state prison.

On the other hand, although the Edwards family inherited abundant capacity and character, every child has been educated from early childhood. Not all of the college members of the family have been discovered, and yet among the men alone I have found 285 graduates and a surprisingly large number of these have supplemented the college course with post-graduate or professional study. Just as the "Jukes" have intensified their degeneracy by neglect, the Edwards family has magnified capacity and character by industry and education.

Among the 285 college graduates of the Edwards family there are thirteen presidents of colleges and other higher institutions of learning, sixty-five professors of colleges, and many principals of important academies and seminaries. Forty-five American and foreign colleges and universities have this family among the alumni. From this family have come presidents for Yale, Princeton, Union, Hamilton, Amherst, the University of California, the University of Tennessee, the famous Litchfield (Conn.) law school, the Columbia law school, and Andover Theological Seminary. Among these are such men as President Timothy Dwight, Yale, 1794-1817; Theodore Dwight Woolsey, Yale, 1846-71; Timothy Dwight, Yale, 1886-97; Jonathan Edwards (Jr.), Union, 1799-1801; Daniel C. Gilman, Johns Hopkins; Merrill E. Gates, Amherst; and Edwards A. Park, Andover.

CHAPTER VII

AARON BURR

Undoubtedly some readers are already impatient at the delay in dealing with Aaron Burr. There was a time when it was the fashion to refer to Colonel Burr as sufficiently infamous to prove that heredity was of no appreciable value. As a matter of fact it is rather refreshing to have one upon whom the imagination can play. It simply intensifies the white light of the rest of the record.

Colonel Burr was not a saint after the model presented by his father, the Rev. Dr. Aaron Burr, the godly president of Princeton; by his grandfather, Jonathan Edwards; or by at least 1,394 of the other members of the family of Mr. Edwards. There is no purpose to give him saintly enthronement, but it may not be amiss to suggest that the abuse of him has been overdone.

Colonel Aaron Burr died at eighty after thirty years of the worst treatment ever meted out to a man against whom the bitterest enemies and the most brilliant legal talent could bring no charge that would stand in the eyes of the law. I have no purpose to lessen the verdict of prejudice, for the study of the Edwards family is all the more fascinating because of one such meteor of error. It must be confessed, however, that a study of the last thirty years of Colonel Burr's life makes one more exasperated with human nature under a political whip than with Colonel Burr's mistake.

At forty-nine Aaron Burr was one of the most brilliant, most admired, and beloved men in the United States. For thirty years his had been a career with few American parallels. He had but one real and intense enemy, and that man had hated him all those years. Alexander Hamilton had never missed an opportunity to vilify Mr. Burr, and his attack had never been resented. Calmly had Aaron Burr pursued his upward and onward course, simply smiling at the vituperation of Hamilton. Could those two men have agreed, they would have been the greatest leaders any nation ever had. Their hatred was as expensive as was that of Blaine and Conklin in after years.

Every age must have a political scapegoat, one upon whose head is placed symbolically the sins of the period, and after he is sent into the wilderness of obscurity it becomes a social and political crime to befriend him. There have been several such in our country's history, and there will be others. Aaron Burr suffered more than any other simply because the glory from which he departed was greater.

On March 2, 1805, Aaron Burr, vice-president of the United States, and president of the senate, retired from the chair two days before his term expired. He made a farewell address, which produced a greater impression upon that body than any other words ever spoken there. Every senator was weeping, and for a long time no one could leave his seat or propose any business. It was a sight for the nation to look upon and wonder. For fourteen years he had been one of the most conspicuous members of that body.

Aaron Burr's ultimate ruin was wrought by his colonization experiment in Louisiana. In popular opinion, there was something traitorous in that unsuccessful venture of his. In 1805 Mr. Burr paid $50,000 for 400,000 acres of land which had been purchased of Spain in 1800, before it passed to France and then to the United States in 1803. Of the motive of Colonel Burr we must always be ignorant; that he was not guilty of any crime in connection therewith we are certain, for the highest tribunal of the land acquitted him. President Jefferson and the entire political force of the administration were bent upon his conviction, but Chief Justice Marshall, as capable, honorable, and incorruptible a jurist as the country has known, would not have it so. Unfortunately, the brilliant arraignment by William Wirt was printed and read for half a century, while the calm rulings of Chief Justice Marshall never went beyond the court room.

Why did a man of his capabilities, upon retirement from the vice-presidency, attempt, at fifty years of age to start life anew under such unpromising conditions? Because he was suddenly politically and professionally ruined. Ruined because he had killed Alexander Hamilton in a duel. Why did he do it? It is a long story.

To make it intelligent, his life must be reviewed. After a brilliant military career, which began when he was nineteen and left him an heroic colonel, he studied law and practiced in Albany. At the age of twenty-eight he was a leader in the New York legislature, and was chairman of the most important committees, always with the people, against the aristocracy—an unpardonable mistake in those times. At thirty-four he was attorney-general of the state, and his great decisions were accepted by all other states. At thirty-four he established the Manhattan bank of New York city. He was the only man with the ability or courage to find a way to establish a bank for the people, and the solidity of that institution for a hundred years is an all-sufficient vindication of his plan. At thirty-five he was appointed and confirmed as a supreme court judge of New York state, but he declined the honor, and was the same year elected to the United States senate. He was re-elected, serving in all fourteen years.

At the second presidential election Senator Burr received one vote in the electoral college, at the third he received thirty, and in the fourth received seventy-three. Jefferson also received seventy-three and the election was thrown into the house. This was in 1800 and Mr. Burr was forty-years of age. The choice lay with New York, which could be carried by no man but Aaron Burr.

Alexander Hamilton was the leader of the Federalists. He also was of New York. It was a battle of the giants. These two men measured swords. The presidency of the United States was the prize both parties—the Federalists and the Democrats—were seeking. New York had always been with the Federalists. In this great struggle it went against Hamilton and for Burr. This ended the political career of Hamilton, and would have done so had he lived longer. He was one of America's greatest statesmen, but one of the poorest politicians. No one could get along with him but Washington, and when he died the political end of Hamilton came.

Jefferson and Burr each received seventy-three votes for president, and Adams received sixty-five. New York had twelve votes, so that if she had remained with the Federalist candidate Adams, he would have won, seventy-seven to sixty-one. This defeat angered Hamilton beyond endurance. He and Burr had been deadly rivals for thirty years, first for the love of woman, then for military preferment, and later in the political arena. When Burr established the Manhattan bank, Hamilton's brother-in-law, inspired by Hamilton, attacked Burr's motive, with the result of a duel in which neither was harmed.

Notwithstanding Hamilton's greatness, he was always in trouble with

31

men and women. He never ceased his abuse of Burr, whose election as senator angered him. Later, when Burr was the choice of congress as minister to Paris, backed especially by Madison and Monroe, Hamilton succeeded in compassing his defeat. Again, when Adams had decided upon some important appointment for Burr, Hamilton succeeded in defeating him. This made Burr's promotion to the vice-presidency and his own downfall the more exasperating to Hamilton.

Four years passed. Burr won high honor as president of the senate, and the party nominated him for governor of New York with practical unanimity. This was too much for Hamilton, who had nothing to lose by indulging his enmity to the full. The campaign against Burr was one of the basest on record. It was one of vilification. Being vice-president, he was at a disadvantage when it came to conducting the campaign, and he was defeated.

There were many features of this campaign that were peculiarly annoying to Burr, and for the second time in his life he resorted to the duel, and Hamilton was killed. Had Burr died in that hour, history would have a different place for him as well as for Hamilton, but in his death Hamilton was glorified. The most preposterous stories, such as his firing into the air, were invented and believed. The time and the conditions were as bad as they could be for Burr. The North never condoned a duel that ended fatally, and then less than ever. I have no word of apology to offer for the duel. It was weakness, as it always is, and from it came all the ills that befell Aaron Burr.

Censure him all you choose, and then look at the conditions of his childhood and wonder that he lived to fifty years of age before the lack of early care brought forth its fruit. Aaron Burr received as good an intellectual and moral legacy as any one of the 1,400 of the Edwards family. His father and mother, grandfather and grandmother would have given him as good an environment and training as any one of them enjoyed, but—his father died before he was two years old, and his mother, grandfather, and grandmother died when he was two years old, and he and his sister, four years old, went to live with his oldest uncle, Timothy Edwards, who was only twenty. This uncle was also bringing up two younger brothers aged eight and thirteen, and three young sisters. While Timothy Edwards made an eminently worthy citizen and reared a family of noble sons and daughters, he was not prepared at nineteen to support so many younger children and give a two-year-old boy the attention that he needed.

At twelve years of age Aaron Burr went to college, and after this time he never had even the apology of a home, indeed he never had a home such as his nature demanded. There are three pictures of the child which satisfy me that the right training would have enabled Aaron Burr to go into history as the noblest Roman of them all.

At four years of age he was at school, where the treatment was so severe that he ran away from school and home and could not be found for three days.

At seven years of age he was up in a cherry tree when a very prim and disagreeable spinster came to call, and he indulged in the childish luxury of throwing cherries at her. She sought "Uncle Timothy," who took the seven-year-old child into the house, gave him a long and severe lecture, offered a long prayer of warning, and then "licked me like a sack."

At ten years of age he ran away from the severity of his uncle, and went to New York and shipped as cabin boy. His uncle followed him, and when the little fellow saw him he went to the top of the masthead and refused to come down until his uncle agreed not to punish him. It is easy to see that his uncle aroused in him all the characteristics that should have been calmed, and gave him none of that care which father or mother would have provided him.

At twelve he entered Princeton, and graduated with honors at sixteen. College life had its temptations, but he conducted himself with unusual decorum, and upon graduation went to study with an eminent clergyman. Apparently he expected to enter the ministry, but the theology of Dr. Bellamy did not commend itself to him, and even less did the spirit with which the theologian met his queries, so that for the remaining sixty odd years of life he would not talk about theology. Here was a brilliant lad, fresh from college, with the inheritance of Burr and Edwards, who might have been led into a glorious career, but was instead repelled, and went back to his uncle's home, with no profession and no plan for life, with no one to advise him.

The battle of Bunker hill aroused Burr to patriotic purpose, and, though but nineteen, he started for Cambridge to enlist. He was stricken with fever, however, and before he was recovered he heard of Arnold's proposed expedition to Quebec, and, though he had better be in bed, he took his musket and walked to Newburyport, 30 miles, in season to ship with the troops. Two men were there ahead of him awaiting his arrival with instructions from his uncle to bring him back to New Jersey. This was too much for young Burr, who did not recognize the right of his uncle to interfere, and he expressed his mind so vigorously as to command the admiration of the soldiers and arouse the fears of the two messengers, who returned without him. This was the last of his uncle's interference. Who that reads of the childhood life of this orphan can wonder that he lacked patience under the severe reverse of political fortune at fifty years of age? That he is the one illustrious exception among the 1,400 need cause no surprise.

CHAPTER VIII

CONTRASTS

It has already been emphasized that the Jukes always mingled blood of their own quality in their descendants, and that the Edwards family has invariably chosen blood of the same general tone and force. Who can think for a moment that the Jukes would have remained on so low a level if the Edwards blood had been mixed with theirs, or that the Edwards would have retained their intellectual supremacy if they had married into the Jukes. The fact is that in 150 years the Jukes never did mingle first-class blood with their own, and the Edwards family has not in 150 years degenerated through marriage.

It is pre-eminently true that a mighty intellectual and moral force does plough the channel of its thought and character through many generations. It would be well for any doubter to study the records of thoroughbreds in the animal world. The highest record ever made for milk and butter was by an animal of no family, and she was valuable only for what she could earn. None of her power went to her offspring. She was simply a high-toned freak, but an animal with a clean pedigree back to some great progenitor is valuable independently of individual earning qualities.

No more would any one claim that the Jukes would not have been immensely improved by education and environment, or that the Edwards family could have maintained its record without education, training, and environment. The facts show that the Jukes first, last, and all the time neglected these advantages, and that the Edwards family, with all its intermarrying, has never neglected them.

The Jukes were notorious law breakers, while the Edwards family has furnished practically no lawbreakers, and a great array of more than 100 lawyers, thirty judges, and the most eminent law professor probably in the country. James Bryce in his comments upon America places one of this family at the head of legal learning on this continent. This was Theodore William Dwight, LL.D., born in New Haven, July 18, 1822; graduated from

Hamilton College, 1840; professor there 1842-58. In 1858 he went to Columbia College, organized the law school and was its president for thirty-three years.

Some of the most eminent official city attorneys of Philadelphia, New York and Chicago have been found in this family. Ex-Governor Hoadley, of Ohio, a descendant of Jonathan Edwards, is now the head of perhaps the leading law firm of New York City or of the country. When one studies the legal side of the family it seems as though they were instinctively and chiefly lawyers and judges. It simply means that whatever the Edwards family has done it has done ably and nobly. There is no greater test of intellectual majesty than that which the practice of law puts upon a man. When James Bryce pays his grand tribute to Dr. Theodore W. Dwight, president of Columbia College law school, it signifies more intellectually than to have said that he was president of the United States.

None of the Jukes had the equivalent of a common school education, while there are few of the Edwards family that have not had more than that. Few were satisfied with less than academy or seminary if they did not go to college. There is not a leading college in the country in which their names are not to be found recorded. They have not only furnished thirteen college presidents and a hundred and more professors, but they have founded many important academies and seminaries in New Haven and Brooklyn, all through the New England states, and in the Middle, Western, and Southern states. They have contributed liberally to college endowments. One gave a quarter of a million as an endowment for Yale.

In Yale alone have been more than 120 graduates. Among these are nearly twenty Dwights, nearly as many Edwards, seven Woolseys, eight Porters, five Johnsons, four Ingersolls, and several of most of the following names: Chapin, Winthrop, Shoemaker, Hoadley, Lewis, Mathers, Reeve, Rowland, Carmalt, Devereaux, Weston, Heermance, Whitney, Blake, Collier, Scarborough, Yardley, Gilman, Raymond, Wood, Morgan, Bacon, Ward, Foote, Cornelius, Shepards, Bristed, Wickerham, Doubleday, Van Volkenberg, Robbins, Tyler, Miller, Lyman, Pierpont, and Churchill, the author of "Richard Carvel," is a recent graduate. In Amherst at one time there were of this family President Gates and Professors Mather, Tyler, and Todd. Wherever found they are leaders even in college faculties. Those who know what Gates, Mather, Tyler, and Todd have stood for as president and professors of Amherst will appreciate what Jonathan Edwards' blood has done for this college.

Of the Jukes, 440 were more or less viciously diseased. The Edwards family was healthy and long lived. Of the eleven children of Mr. and Mrs. Edwards, four lived to be more than seventy years of age,—seventy-three, seventy-five, seventy-seven and seventy-nine,—and three others were fifty, fifty-six, and sixty-three. Only one died unmarried, none died in childhood. The record for health and longevity continues through every generation. They have also done much to alleviate the sufferings of mankind. There have been sixty physicians, all marked men. Dr. Richard Smith Dewey was an eminent surgeon in the Franco-Prussian war, having charge of the Prussian hospital at Hesse Cassel. Dr. Sereno Edwards Dwight was a physician and surgeon in the British regular army. The physicians of the family have had important connection with insane asylums and hospitals. The legislative action of New York, by which the first insane asylum of the state was built, was largely the result of a physician of this family. The medical superintendent of the Illinois state insane asylum was another of the family. Eminent names in the medical annals of San Francisco, Chicago, Detroit, New York, Boston, and other cities can be traced to Jonathan Edwards.

The Jukes neglected all religious privileges, defied and antagonized the church and all that it stands for, while the Edwards family has more than a 100 clergymen, missionaries, and theological professors, many of the most eminent in the country's history. America has had no more brilliant preachers and theologians than some of those that bear the names of Edwards, Dwight, Woolsey, Park, Ingersoll. There have been no more noted missionaries than this family has sent for faithful and successful work in Asia Minor, India, Africa, China, Hawaii, and the South Sea islands. Dwight's famous five volumes on theology are a product of a worthy descendant of Jonathan Edwards. Edwards A. Park, the longtime head of Andover theological seminary, whose vigor of thought, keenness of logic, and pulpit power are unsurpassed, was a descendant of Mr. Edwards. The family has furnished several army chaplains and one eminent chaplain of the United States senate. They have made many churches prominent for the vigor of their pulpit utterances. The famous Second church, Portland, Park street church of

37

Boston, and many in New Haven and other Connecticut cities and towns as well as many churches in the Middle and Western States owe much to the descendants of Mr. Edwards.

Not one of the Jukes was ever elected to a public office, while more than eighty of the family of Jonathan Edwards have been especially honored. Legislatures in all sections of the country, governor's councils, state treasuries, and other elective offices have been filled by these men. They have been mayors of New Haven, Cleveland, and Troy; governors of Connecticut, Ohio, and South Carolina; they have been prominent in the Continental congress, in the constitutional conventions of Massachusetts, Connecticut, New York, Ohio, Illinois, and Wisconsin. They have represented the United States at several foreign courts; several have been members of congress; three have been United States senators, and one vice-president of the United States.

The Jukes lacked the physical and moral courage, as well as the patriotic purpose, to enlist, but there were seventy-five officers in the army and navy from the family of Mr. Edwards. This family has been prominent as officers, chaplains, or surgeons, in the army and navy in the three great wars. In the Civil war they were at Shiloh, New Orleans, and with the Red river expedition, at Fort Fisher and Newbern, at Big Bethel, Antietam, and Gettysburg, on Lookout mountain with Hooker, with Sheridan in the Shenandoah, and were on the march to the sea with Sherman.

One spinster of the family residing in Detroit expressed much regret that she had no husband. The reason she gave, however, was highly complimentary to the sterner sex,—because she had no husband to send to the Civil war. Having none, she paid the regulation bounty and had a man in the service of her country for three years in lieu of the husband she would have sent if she had had one.

The Jukes were as far removed as possible from literature. They not only never created any, but they never read anything that could by any stretch of the imagination be styled good reading. In the Edwards family some sixty have attained prominence in authorship or editorial life. "Richard Carvel," is by Mr. Winston Churchill, a descendant of Mr. Edwards, and I have found 135 books of merit written by the family. Eighteen considerable journals and periodicals have been edited and several important ones founded by the

Edwards family.

The Jukes did not wander far from the haunts of Max. They stagnated like the motionless pool, while the Edwards family is a prominent factor in the mercantile, industrial, and professional life of thirty-three states of the union and in several foreign countries, in ninety-two American and many foreign cities. They have been pre-eminently directors of men. The Pacific steamship line and fifteen American railway systems have had as president, superintendent, or otherwise active in the management one of this family. Many large banks, banking houses, and insurance companies have been directed by them. They have been owners or superintendents of large coal mines in Pennsylvania and West Virginia, of large iron plants and vast oil interests in Pennsylvania, and of silver mines in Nevada. There is scarcely any great American industry that has not had one of this family among its chief promoters. Eli Whitney of cotton-gin fame married a granddaughter of Jonathan Edwards.

Prison reform has found its leading advocates in this family. Wilberforce's best American friend was of this fold, and Garibaldi valued one of the family above all other American supporters.

Whatever the Jukes stand for, the Edwards family does not. Whatever weakness the Jukes represent finds its antidote in the Edwards family, which has cost the country nothing in pauperism, in crime, in hospital or asylum service. On the contrary, it represents the highest usefulness in invention, manufacture, commerce, founding of asylums and hospitals, establishing and developing missions, projecting and energizing the best philanthropies.

CHAPTER IX

TIMOTHY EDWARDS

To make more clear, if possible, the persistence of intellectual activity and moral virtue, let us study samples of the family. Take for instance the eldest son, Timothy. He was a member of and leader in the famous Massachusetts council of war in the Revolution, a colonel in the militia, and a judge. His descendants have been leaders in Binghamton, Pittsburg, Indianapolis, Bangor, St. Louis, Northampton, New Bedford, San Francisco, New York, New Haven, and many other cities and towns in New England, New York, Pennsylvania, West Virginia, and Ohio. From his descendants a Connecticut town, Chaplin, is named; Newark, Ohio, had a long-time principal, Jonathan E. Chaplin; Andover Theological Seminary had one of its most famous treasurers, Samuel Farrar; the American board of missions had one of its grandest leaders and secretaries, Dr. Elias Cornelius; the American Baptist Missionary Union had one of its eminent secretaries, Dr. Solomon Peck; the American Missionary Association had as its great treasurer, W.E. Whiting; the famous young ladies' seminary of Lenox, Mass., had for thirty years its great principal, Elizabeth Sedgwick; Boston had a prominent lawyer, a graduate of Harvard, William Minot; St. Louis had a leading lawyer, William D. Sedgwick; Antietam had in the list of killed the gallant Major Sedgwick; San Francisco recorded among her distinguished sons the long-time superintendent of the Pacific mail steamship company; the United States navy counted as one of her able officers a surgeon, Dr. George Hopkins; Amherst had as her most famous instructor Professor W.S. Tyler, D.D., LL.D., at the head of the Greek department for half a century; she also has the present brilliant professor of biology, John M. Tyler; Sheridan had as a brilliant colonel in the grand ride of the Shenandoah Colonel M.W. Tyler; invention claims the discoverer of the Turbine wheel, W.W. Tyler; Knox College has claimed as a leader at one time, as has Smith at another, Professor Henry H. Tyler.

A detailed study of the family of the eldest son is suggestive. He was the sixth child, born in Northampton, 1738, when the father was thirty-five and the mother twenty-eight. He was but twenty years old when the father and mother died and the care of the family devolved upon him. He had graduated from Princeton the previous year but the responsibility of a large family prevented his entering upon professional life. Two years after the death of his father he married and removed to Elizabethtown, N.J., where he resided for ten years. In 1770 he returned to Stockbridge, Mass. Berkshire county was still on the frontier and was sparsely settled. The store which Mr. Edwards opened in 1770 was the first in the county. The settlers raised wheat on the newly cleared land. This Mr. Edwards bought and sent to New York, bringing back goods in return. In five years he became the most prosperous man in the county, buying and clearing a very large farm on which he employed as many as fifty men in the busy season.

The outbreak of the Revolutionary struggle was a most inopportune time for Timothy Edwards; but for that he would have become one of the wealthiest men of his day. All business was suspended and he gave himself to his country's cause with intense devotion. He was at once appointed on a commission with General Schuyler to treat with the Indians; was appointed commissary to look after the supply of the army with provisions. From 1777 to 1780 he was a leader in the Legislature of Massachusetts; was elected to the Continental Congress with John Hancock and John Adams; was a colonel in the Massachusetts militia and a judge of probate. When the war broke out Timothy Edwards was worth $20,000, which he had accumulated in addition to all his other burdens. When the war closed he had nothing, and was $3,000 in debt to New York merchants. To understand what sacrifices he made it must be understood that when the government was in great straits he took $5,000 of money that was as good as gold and let the government have it, taking in return money that was of slight value. He also took fifty tons of flour to Springfield and let the government have it for paper money at par. There were no greater heroes in the Revolutionary war than such men as Timothy Edwards. He was nearly fifty years old when the war closed and he found himself the father of thirteen children and without property or business. Full of courage and enterprise he succeeded in supporting his family in comfort and in regaining a substantial property before his death, which occurred in the midst of the next war, October 27, 1813.

It was not an easy thing to educate children in those times. When the Revolutionary war broke out his oldest child was but thirteen, and when it ended he had ten children under twenty-one. There were only three books in the schools at Stockbridge during the war, Dilworth's Spelling Book and Arithmetic and the Book of Psalms. From these the children of Timothy Edwards received their education and that it was a good training subsequent events show.

The first born, a daughter, married Benjamin Chaplin, Jr., a graduate of Yale (1778), and for her second husband Capt. Dan Tyler, of Brookline, Ct., a graduate of Harvard. Her second child, Edward, became Register of Probate. Jonathan, the second born, had several children who became prominent in professional and business life. Phoebe married Rev. Asahel Hooker, an eminent graduate of Yale, and for her second husband Rev. Samuel Farrer, a graduate of Harvard, and for many years treasurer and financial agent of Andover Theological Seminary. Her children were noted men and women, graduates of Yale and Dartmouth, clergymen, theological professors, secretary of the American Board of Foreign Missions, and secretary American Baptist Missionary Union, prominent teachers and authors.

Rhoda Edwards, another of Timothy's daughters, married Col. Josiah Dwight, of Springfield. Among their fifteen children and their descendants are the founder of a famous young ladies' school at Lenox; an author of "Spanish Conquest of America," and five other considerable works; clerk of supreme court of Massachusetts; a Boston lawyer, graduate of Harvard; an eminent linguist and graduate of Harvard; music teacher in New York City, educated in Germany; St. Louis lawyer, graduate of Harvard college and law school, who studied in Germany; major in Civil war, wounded at Antietam; hospital nurse in Civil war; graduate of Yale; graduate of Cambridge, Eng., and author of "Five Years in an English University;" a graduate of Amherst and Andover, and missionary in Southern India; lawyer in Springfield; eminent teacher at Northampton; leading physician at Northampton; leading physician at New Bedford; supt. Pacific Mail Steamship Company; merchant in New York; insurance manager, New York; author of "Greece and Roman Mythology," and five other important works; supt. Cincinnati, Hamilton & Dayton R.R.; a New York lawyer and graduate of Yale; author of "History of

Virginia," and two other works; graduate Dartmouth and Andover; assistant surgeon U.S. Navy; and an officer in Civil war, who fought in thirty battles.

Mary Edwards, another daughter of Timothy, married Mason Whiting, District Attorney of New York, and member of New York Legislature. In this family of eight children and their descendants are an authoress; a colonel in Civil war; treasurer American Missionary Association; Rev. W.S. Tyler, D.D., LL.D., a graduate of Amherst and Andover, professor of Greek for fifty years at Amherst; Col. Mason Whiting Tyler, graduate of Amherst, gallant soldier in Civil war; Wm. W. Tyler, graduate of Amherst, manufacturer of famous Turbine Water Wheels; Henry Mather Tyler, graduate of Amherst, professor of Greek at Knox College, pastor at Galesburg, Fitchburg and Worcester, and professor of Greek at Smith College; John Mason Tyler, graduate of Amherst and Union Theological Seminary, studied at Gothenburg and Leipsic, professor of Biology at Amherst and eminent lecturer.

To William Edwards, another son of Timothy, oldest son of Jonathan Edwards, an entire chapter will be given.

CHAPTER X

COLONEL WILLIAM EDWARDS

Fascinating is the story of Colonel William Edwards, grandson of Jonathan Edwards, the inventor of the process of tanning by which the leather industry of the world was revolutionized. In no respect did the intellectual and moral inheritance show itself more clearly than in the recuperative force of the family of Colonel Edwards.

Attention has already been called to the remarkable way in which the father, Timothy Edwards, re-established himself and educated his large family after his great financial reverses in the period of the Revolutionary war, but the story of Colonel William Edwards is even a more striking illustration of this same power. He was born at Elizabeth, New Jersey, November 11, 1770. He was a mere child during the Revolutionary struggle. Before he was two years old the father removed to Stockbridge, Mass., and the boy grew up in as thoroughly a rural community as could be found. The school privileges were very meagre. No books were printed in the American colonies because of British prohibition. From early childhood he had to work, first as his mother's assistant, tending the children and doing all kinds of household work such as a handy boy can do. As soon as he could sit on a horse he rode for light ploughing and by the time he was ten was driving oxen for heavy ploughing and teaming.

William Edwards was only thirteen when he was put out as an apprentice to a tanner in Elizabethtown, N.J. To reach this place the lad had to ride horseback to the Hudson river, about thirty miles, make arrangements to have the horse taken back, and take passage on a West Indies cattle brig to New York. It took him a week to get to New York. He then took the ferry for Elizabethtown.

When young Edwards began life as a tanner it took twelve months for the tanning of hides. This was by far the most extensive tannery in America. It had a capacity of 1,500 sides. The only "improvement" then known—1784—was the use of a wooden plug in the lime vats and water

44

pools to let off the contents into the brook. The bark was ground by horse power. There was a curb fifteen feet in diameter, made of three-inch plank, with a rim fifteen inches high. Within this was a stone wheel with many hollows and the wooden wheel with long pegs. Two horses turned these wheels which would grind half a cord of bark in a day of twelve hours. The first year William was at work grinding bark. All the pay received for the year's work was the knowledge gained of the art of grinding bark, very poor board (no clothing, no money), and the privilege of tanning for himself three sheep skins. The fourth half year he received his first money, $2.50 a month, which was paid out of friendliness for the Edwards family.

Before he was twenty he set up in business for himself. He had saved $100; his father, still poor, gave him $300; he bought land for his plant for $700 on long credit. After years of great struggle he succeeded in business and developed the process by which instead of employing one hand for every one hundred sides he could tan 40,000 with twenty lads and the cost was reduced from twelve cents a pound to four cents. The quality was improved even more than the cost was reduced. When the war of 1812 broke out he had practically the only important tannery in the United States, but the war scare and attendant evils led to his failure in 1815. He was now 45 years old with a wife and nine children. He went to work in a factory for day wages to keep his family supplied with the necessities of life. By some misunderstanding and a combination of law suits his patents were lost to him.

When Colonel Edwards failed in 1815 he owed considerable sums of money and nine years later the courts released him from all obligations, yet between the age of 69 and 75 he paid every cent of this indebtedness amounting to $25,924.

The chief interest in Colonel Edwards centers in his children. When his failure came there were nine children, five boys and four girls. The youngest was a few months old and the eldest 19. Seven of them were under 12 years of age. In the first four years of their reverses two others were born, so that his large family had their preparation and start in life in the years of struggle. Nevertheless they took their places among the prosperous members of the Edwards family. The eldest son, William W. Edwards, was one of the eminently successful men of New York. He lived to be 80 years old and his life was fully occupied with good work. He was engaged in the straw goods business in New York; helped to develop the insurance business to large proportions; organized the Dime Savings Bank of Brooklyn, of which he was treasurer and cashier. He was one of the founders of the American Tract Society and of the New York Mercantile Library. He was a member of the State legislature for several terms.

Henry Edwards was one of Boston's most eminent merchants and a most useful man. He had the only strictly wholesale silk house in Boston for nearly half a century. He was born in Northampton, 1798. At the age of fifteen he entered the employ of a prominent Boston importing house and began by opening the store, building the fires, and carrying out goods. By the time he was twenty he was the most trusted employee. He was a born trader. His brother in New York knowing that twist buttons were scarce in that city suggested that Henry buy up all there were in Boston before the dealers discovered the fact that they were scarce in New York and send them on to him. They cleared $500 in a few weeks. He was an earnest student. Not having had the advantages of an education he made up for it by studying evenings. They imported their silks from France which led him to study French until he was accomplished in the art of reading and speaking the French language. It is rather remarkable that learning the language in this way, he was able to go to France and out-rank most foreigners in Parisian society. An Edwards did not absolutely need the college and the university in order to be eminently scholarly in any special line.

At the age of twenty-five he went into business as the senior partner of the house of Edwards & Stoddard on State street, Boston. It was the only house that made its whole business the importing of silks. At the age of twenty-eight he went to Paris to purchase silks and remained there many years. They did a highly profitable business for nearly fifty years. He received much social attention while in Paris. General Lafayette was specially friendly, and the families visited frequently. He was also highly honored in Boston, where he was a member of the city government—it was an honor in those days—for nine years, one of the trustees of Amherst College for forty years, a member of the Massachusetts legislature and received several important appointments of trust and honor from Governor John A. Andrew and President Lincoln. Boston had few men in his day who were more prosperous or more highly honored.

Ogden E. Edwards was for several years at the head of one of the largest leather houses of New York City, eminently prosperous and of great service to the public. Alfred Edwards was founder and senior partner in one of the largest wholesale dry goods houses of New York for fifty years, known as Alfred Edwards & Co. Amory was for many years a member of the firm of Alfred Edwards & Co. He was also United States Consul at Buenos Ayres, and traveled extensively in South America. His nephew, Wm. H. Edwards, wrote of these travels. This nephew, resident at Coalbough, West Virginia, is the author of a famous work on "The Butterflies of North America," and also of an important work on "Shaksper nor Shakespeare." Richard C. Edwards was also a member of the firm of Alfred Edwards & Co. and shared the prosperity of the house with his brother.

Rebecca T. Edwards, the eldest daughter, married Benjamin Curtis, a wealthy merchant in business in New York and Paris. She was married in Paris and General Lafayette gave her away in place of her father. Sarah H. Edwards married Rev. John N. Lewis, a successful clergyman. Elizabeth T. Edwards married Henry Rowland, an eminently successful and useful citizen of New York, whose children, like himself, have been honored in many ways.

Ann Maria Edwards married Professor Edwards A. Park, D.D., the president of Andover Theological Seminary and the most eminent theologian of the day. Their son, Rev. William Edwards Park, of Gloversville, New York, is a preacher of rare ability. Rev. W.E. Park has two sons, graduates of Yale, young men of great promise.

The ten children of Colonel Edwards lived to great age, and each of the sons was eminently successful in business, and all were highly esteemed. Each of the daughters married men eminent in commercial or professional life. None of them were privileged to receive a liberal education because of the great financial reverses that came to the father in their youth, but every one of them was closely identified with educational institutions and all were rated as scholarly men and women.

CHAPTER XI

THE MARY EDWARDS DWIGHT FAMILY

After studying at some length the family of the eldest son of Jonathan Edwards, it is worth while to study the family of one of the daughters. Mary, the fourth child born at Northampton (1734), was married at the age of 16 to Timothy Dwight, born in Vermont (1726) and graduated from Yale in 1744.

It is interesting to find a daughter of Jonathan Edwards marrying a Yale graduate, who "had such extreme sensibility to the beauty and sweetness of always doing right, and such a love of peace, and regarded the legal profession as so full of temptations to do wrong, in great degree and small" that he persistently refused to study law, though it had been his father's great desire. The conscientiousness of Major Dwight is well illustrated by this incident. There was a lottery in the interest of Princeton college, authorized by the legislature of New Jersey, and Dwight was sent twenty tickets for sale. He returned them, but the time required for the mail in those days was so long that they did not reach the destination until after the drawing. Major Dwight was notified that one of his twenty tickets had drawn $20,000 and all but one ticket had drawn some prize. Major Dwight paid for the one blank ticket and would not take a cent of the large prize money. This was worthy a son-in-law of Mr. Edwards, the progenitor of a family of mighty men.

Major Dwight was a merchant in Northampton, a selectman, judge of probate for sixteen years and was for several years a member of the legislature. At the time of his death, 1778, he was possessed of 3,000 acres of valuable land in Northampton, and he willed his wife $7,050, and each of his thirteen children $1,165. At that time there were but five painted houses in Northampton and but two were carpeted. Of the fourteen children, thirteen grew up, and twelve were married; and their entire family adds greatly to the glory of the family of Jonathan Edwards. The oldest son, Dr. Timothy Dwight, president of Yale, said with much tenderness and force, "All that I am and all that I shall be, I owe to my mother." She was a woman of remarkable will power and intellectual vigor. She was but seventeen when her first child was born and was the mother of fourteen children at forty-two.

The first-born, President Timothy Dwight, S.T.D., LL.D., born 1752, was one of the most eminent of Americans. He learned his alphabet at a single sitting while a mere child, and at four knew the catechism by heart. He graduated from Yale at seventeen; taught the Hopkins school in New Haven at seventeen and eighteen; was tutor in Yale from nineteen to twenty-five years of age; wrote the "Conquest of Canada," which was reprinted in London, at nineteen. This work was dedicated to George Washington by permission. At twenty-three, he was in the fore front of the advocates of independence. At twenty-two, General Washington appointed him a chaplain in the army, and personally requested that he accept. His widow received $350 a year pension because of this service. He was a member of the Massachusetts legislature and secured an important grant to Harvard university. He was offered a professorship at Harvard and could have gone to Congress without opposition, but he declined both, and at thirty-two accepted a country pastorate at Greenfield Hill, Connecticut. He remained there twenty-two years. His salary was $750. He also had a gift of $1,500 for accepting the call, a parish lot of six acres, and twenty cords of wood annually. This was said to be the largest ministerial salary in New England. At forty-three he was called from the country parish to the presidency of Yale. His salary as president was $334. Later he had $500, from which he paid $150 for two amanuenses which he required because his sight had failed him. He published fourteen important works. He was largely instrumental in organizing the American Board of Commissioners of Foreign Missions; the American Missionary Society and the American Bible Society. To him is largely due the establishment of theological seminaries in the country. For forty-six years he taught every year either in a public or private school or college, and all but one year of that time he preached every week and almost invariably he prepared a new sermon. When he died, from a cancer at sixty-five, the children insisted that the estate should be for the mother during her lifetime, and when she died there was found to be $26,000 although his salary had always been ridiculously small.

The eight children were all boys, and all but one grew to manhood. Timothy was a hardware merchant in New Haven and New York for more than forty years. He endowed the "Dwight Professorship of Didactic

49

Theology in Yale," which was named for him. There were nine children, grandchildren of President Dwight by his eldest son. Of these the eldest, also Timothy, was the leading paper manufacturer in the trust mill headquarters at Chicago, and his six children were enterprising and successful business men in Illinois and Wisconsin. John William Dwight was one of the leading manufacturers of chemicals in Connecticut. Edward Strong Dwight, of Yale, 1838, and of Theological Seminary, Yale, was for many years a trustee of Amherst and a prominent clergyman. J.H. Lyman, M.D., and Edward Huntington Lyman, M.D., were names that added luster to the family of President Dwight. Benjamin Woolsey Dwight, M.D., another son of the President of Yale, was a graduate of Yale and treasurer of Hamilton college for nineteen years. Among his descendants are Richard Smith Dewey, M.D., of Ann Arbor, in charge of Brooklyn City Hospital; charge of military hospital at Hesse Cassel in Franco-Prussian war; assistant superintendent Illinois State Insane hospital at Elgin. Also Elliott Anthony, of Hamilton, 1850; Chicago lawyer; city attorney; a member of the Illinois Constitutional Convention in 1862 and again in 1870; founder of the Law Institute, Chicago, and for several years the president. Also Edward Woolsey Dwight, who was a leading citizen and legislator of Wisconsin.

It is impracticable to give the record of many of the distinguished members of such a family, but a brief notice of a few will give some idea of the standard of the family.

Benj. Woodbridge Dwight, Ph.D., b. 1816, g. Hamilton 1835, Yale Theological Seminary, professor in Hamilton; founded Central Presbyterian church, Joliet, Ill.; established "Dwight's High School," Brooklyn; editor-in-chief of "The Interior" of Chicago, which he owned and edited; contributor to many magazines; author of several scholarly works; had the first preparatory school which placed German on a level with Greek in importance, and founded a large preparatory boarding school at Clinton, N.Y. He was a man of rare ability, character and success.

Prof. Theodore William Dwight, LL.D., b. 1822, g. Hamilton 1840, g. Yale Law S.; professor Hamilton College sixteen years; dean of Columbia College Law S. from 1858 to 1892. James Brice of England placed him at the head of legal learning in the United States and said: "It would be worth an English student's while to cross the Atlantic to attend his course." Another eminent English lawyer, A.V. Dicey, in "Legal Education" wrote of him as "the greatest living American teacher of law." He gave a course of lectures each year at Cornell; was a member of the N.Y. Constitutional Convention in 1867; was a member of the famous committee of seventy in N.Y. City that exposed the Tweed ring; was president of the New York Prison Association and presided when Mr. Dugdale was employed to study the Jukes; associate editor "American Law Register;" was legal editor of "Johnson's Encyclopædia," and made many important contributions to the legal literature of the country. There have been few men of equal eminence in our country's history.

President Theodore Dwight Woolsey, D.D., LL.D., b. New York City, October 31, 1801, was the grandson of Mary Edwards Dwight and great grandson of Jonathan Edwards; g. Yale 1820; studied at Princeton Theological Seminary and g. at Yale L.S.; studied in German universities; professor in Yale twenty-two years; president of Yale 1846-1871. Wesleyan conferred degree of LL.D. and Harvard that of LL.D. and S.T.D. all before he was fifty years of age. President of the Evangelical Alliance held in N.Y. City 1873, the leading American on the Committee for the Revision of the Bible. After resigning the presidency he continued to lecture at Yale until his death, 1889. There was no more eminent American in unofficial life from 1840 to 1890 than he. President Hayes once said that he was greatly perplexed at one time as to the line of public policy which he should pursue until it occurred to him that President Woolsey was the one American on whose judgment he could rely, and after consulting him his course was entirely clear and his action wise. He was the author of several valuable and standard works. Yale's first great advance was in the time of President Timothy Dwight, its second was in the administration of President Theodore Dwight Woolsey. When he became president the classes about doubled in size. He introduced new departments at once and endowments came in, such as had never been considered possible. The tuition was raised from $33 to $90; the salaries were greatly increased, graduate courses were introduced; many new buildings were erected and everything went forward at a radically different pace. Yale and American thought owe much to President Woolsey. He wrote many scholarly works.

There were thirteen children born to President Woolsey. Of these,

51

one daughter married Rev. Edgar Laing Heermance, a graduate of Yale and a useful and talented man; one of the sons, Theodore Salisbury, was a graduate of Yale, and professor of International Law at Yale.

President Timothy Dwight, D.D., LL.D., b. 1828, g. Yale 1849, g. Yale Theological School, studied at Bonn and Berlin in Germany; was professor at Yale and president from 1886 to 1897. He has been an eminent American scholar for half a century. If there were but two or three such men in a family it would make it memorable. Yale gave him the degree of D.D., and both Harvard and Princeton that of LL.D. He was editor of "The New Englander." It is a singular fact that the three great advances which Yale has made have been in the times of the two Dwights and of Woolsey, all descendants of Jonathan Edwards. By the end of his third year the number of students had risen to 1365 and the sixth year to 1784. The gifts to Yale in each of the fifteen years of his administration were fabulous as compared with any past experiences, often above $350,000.

President Sereno Edwards Dwight, D.D., g. Yale 1803, practiced law in New Haven; author of important books which were republished in England; became a clergyman at the age of twenty-nine; pastor of Park St. Church, Boston; was chaplain of the U.S. Senate; established successful boarding school in New Haven. Among his students were the two boys who afterwards made the famous Andrews & Stoddard's Latin Grammar. His literary work was extensive and valuable. Standing by himself he would shed lustre upon the names he bore, Edwards and Dwight. He was a tutor in Yale and was third president of Hamilton College.

William Theodore Dwight, D.D., b. 1795, g. Yale 1813, tutor at Yale, practiced law in Philadelphia; became a clergyman; pastor in Portland; overseer of Bowdoin College. He was offered three professorships, which he declined. He was one of the religious leaders of America for many years.

Hon. Theodore Dwight, b. 1764, lawyer. Editor "The Connecticut Mirror" and "The Hartford Courant;" member of Congress, where he won honors by successfully combating the famous John Randolph; secretary of the famous Hartford Convention; established and edited 1815-17 the "Albany Daily Advertiser;" established and edited the "New York Daily Advertiser" 1817-36; wrote "Life of Thomas Jefferson," and many other works of importance. There were few men in his day who occupied a position of such influence.

Theodore Dwight, 2d, b. 1796, g. Yale 1814, eminent scholar, imprisoned in Paris for distributing the New Testament gratis in the streets; spoke seven languages; was the warmest American friend of Garibaldi and was authorized by him to edit his works in this country; was director N.Y. Asylum for the Blind, and of the N.Y. Public School Assn.; was instrumental in having music introduced into the schools of N.Y. City; was prominent in religious and philanthropic as well as educational work. In the Kansas crisis he induced 3,000 settlers to go to Kansas, and indirectly caused nearly 10,000 to go at that critical time. He edited at various times "The N.Y. Daily Advertiser," "The Youths Penny Paper," "The American Magazine," "The Family Visitor," "The N.Y. Presbyterian," "The Christian Alliance," and wrote several successful text-books and many literary and historical works. He was a leader in the noblest sense of the term.

Nathaniel Dwight, M.D., b. 1770, surgeon in United States Army, practiced medicine in Providence; prepared the first school geography ever published in the United States; wrote many historical works; original advocate of special institutional care for the insane. After eleven years of ardent championship he saw the first insane retreat established.

Henry E. Dwight, M.D., b. 1832, g. Yale 1852, g. Andover Theological Seminary 1857, studied in Germany and France and was an eminent physician in Philadelphia. Rev. S.G. Dwight, g. Union Theological Seminary, and was a missionary in the Sandwich Islands.

Here are a few who can only be named: John W. Dwight, b. 1820, g. Yale, eminent divine and trustee of Amherst College for many years.

Mrs. Rensselaer Nicol, of New Haven, a leader in prison reform and other philanthropic movements.

Thomas B. Dwight, b. 1857, g. Yale, district attorney of Philadelphia and eminent lawyer.

Sereno E. Dwight, surgeon in British army.

James A. Dwight, b. 1855, in United States navy.

Samuel H. Stunner was with Sherman in his march to the sea.

Mrs. R.H. Perkins, b. 1819, eminent teacher, principal Duffield school, Detroit.

William H. Sumner, officer in U.S. regular army.

53

Thomas Berry, banker in Cleveland.

General Robert Montgomery, of Pennsylvania.

O.H. Kennedy, officer in U.S. navy.

Fenton Rockwell, judge advocate and provost judge in New Orleans; officer in Civil war, and in many important battles.

William R. Dwight, New York banker.

George S. Dwight, large railroad contractor.

William Allerton, leather merchant in Boston.

Mrs. Egbert C. Smyth, wife of the dean of Andover Theological Seminary.

Rossiter W. Raymond, eminent specialist, author, and lecturer.

W.M. Bell, manufacturer, Allegheny.

Colonel A.S.M. Morgan, U.S.A.

J.E. Jacobs, insurance manager, Chicago.

E.S. Churchill, Portland, Me., merchant.

W.D. Bell, manufacturer, Philadelphia.

George Collier, rich St. Louis banker.

E.A. Hitchcock, tea merchant, Hong Kong.

M.D. Collier, graduated from Yale; St. Louis lawyer.

H.R. Bell, Chicago physician.

D.W. Bell, Pittsburg lawyer.

A.S. Bell, Pittsburg lawyer.

George Hoadley, born in 1781; graduated from Yale; mayor New Haven; eight times mayor of Cleveland.

W.W. Hoadley, born in 1814; Cincinnati banker.

Dr. T.F. Pomeroy, Detroit.

General J.H. Bates, U.S.A.; Ohio state senate.

Governor George Hoadley, born in 1826; graduated from Western Reserve College; supreme court judge; president Democratic convention that nominated General Hancock for the presidency.

Major W.W. Winthrop of the Civil war; graduated from Tale.

Major W.T. Johnson, graduated from Yale; killed at battle of Big Bethel.

Theodore Weston, graduated from Yale; civil engineer of Croton water works.

J.M. Woolsey, born in 1796; graduated from Yale; capitalist, Cleveland.

Sarah C. Woolsey is "Susan Coolidge."

Mrs. Daniel C. Grilman, wife of the president of Johns Hopkins University, and formerly president of University of California.

Samuel Carmalt, wealthy land owner in Pennsylvania.

Dr. W.W. Woolsey, born in 1831; graduated from Yale; physician, Dubuque, Ia.

T.B. Woolsey, flour merchant, New York.

Samuel W. Johnson, graduated from Princeton and Harvard law school; New York lawyer.

Woolsey Johnson, M.D., graduated from Princeton and New York Medical College; physician, New York.

Theodore S. Woolsey, graduated from Yale; professor in Yale.

Charles F. Johnson, graduated from Yale; professor United States Naval Academy, Annapolis.

W.W. Johnson, graduated from Yale; professor Kenyon College.

J.H. Rathburn, lawyer, Utica.

J.O. Pease, merchant, Philadelphia.

A.S. Dwight, lieutenant U.S.A.; killed at Petersburg.

George P.B. Dwight, New York custom house.

Henry E. Dwight, born in 1813; Southern planter.

Theodore Woolsey Porter, b. 1799, g. Yale 1819, eminent teacher; principal of Washington Institute, New York City.

Timothy Dwight Porter, M.D., b. 1797, g. Yale 1816, was in the New York senate and a successful practitioner.

Imperfectly as these names represent the achievements of the descendants of Mary Edwards Dwight they do hint strongly at the vigor, character and scholarship for which the family of Jonathan Edwards stands in American life.

There is another large family of Dwights, direct descendants of Jonathan Edwards, through his granddaughter, Rhoda Edwards, but these are not, of course, included in this list of Mary's descendants. Many of these are eminent men, and reference is here made to their omission, lest some one should think the facts regarding them were not gathered.

A MODERN INSTANCE

It was known that John Eliot Woodbridge removed to Youngstown, O., about one hundred years ago, but no trace of him was found until these chapters were in type when it appeared that this undiscovered remainder was a most important branch of the family.

Congressman R.W. Taylor, of Ohio, chairman of the committee to pass upon the case of Mr. Roberts of Utah, is a descendant of Jonathan Edwards through John Eliot Woodbridge. His masterly treatment of the case is recognized throughout the country. Here is what the "Detroit Free Press" said of him at the time of the investigation:

"In appearance he is not of the robust order of statesmen. With fair face, shoulders that he has always permitted to droop, indispensable eyeglasses, and hands that nine women out of ten would envy, modest demeanor, and kindly instincts, he is among the last of men that a casual observer would pick as fitting leaders where nerve, aggressiveness, and fearless determination must be joined with an ability to give and take in legal controversy.

"But this passing judgment would be at widest variance with the truth. College mates of Taylor will recall the deceptiveness of this outward appearance. It concealed muscles of steel and a will that had only to be right in order to be invincible. He was the peer of any amateur baseball catcher in his day, and held the same enviable place as a student of the classics. He was the strong man for the D.K.E. initiations, and took the same rank in all scholastic competitions."

Dr. Timothy Woodbridge, of Youngstown, was a graduate of the medical college of Philadelphia, and was one of the eminent physicians of Eastern Ohio. His grandson, Benjamin Warner Wells, of Chicago, was a graduate of Annapolis naval academy. He was Admiral Schley's flag secretary in the engagement at Santiago. Dr. John Eliot Woodbridge, Cleveland, is an eminent specialist in typhoid fever cases. Robert Walker Taylor was comptroller of the United States treasury for fifteen years.

www.ingramcontent.com/pod-product-compliance
Lightning Source LLC
Chambersburg PA
CBHW071249280526
45788CB00004B/1644